Library and Archives Canada Cataloguing in Publication

Khan, Ausma Zehanat, author
Ramadan: the holy month of fasting / Ausma Zehanat Khan.
(Orca origins)

Includes bibliographical references and index.

ISBN 978-1-4598-1181-2 (hardcover).—ISBN 978-1-4598-1182-9 (pdf).—ISBN 978-1-4598-1183-6 (epub)

1. Ramadan—Juvenile literature. I. Title.
BP186.4.K45 2018   j297.3'62   c2017-904562-8
                          c2017-904563-6

First published in the United States, 2018
Library of Congress Control Number: 2017949708

Summary: Part of the nonfiction Orca Origins series for middle readers. Illustrated with color photographs,
this book examines the origins and traditions of the Muslim holy month of Ramadan.

*Orca Book Publishers is dedicated to preserving the environment and has
printed this book on Forest Stewardship Council® certified paper.*

Orca Book Publishers gratefully acknowledges the support for its publishing programs provided by the
following agencies: the Government of Canada through the Canada Book Fund and the Canada Council for the Arts,
and the Province of British Columbia through the BC Arts Council and the Book Publishing Tax Credit.

Edited by Sarah N. Harvey
Designed by Rachel Page
Front cover photos by Athif Ali Khan, iStock.com/ingerszz and iStock.com/FOTOKITA
Back cover photo by iStock.com

ORCA BOOK PUBLISHERS
www.orcabook.com

Printed and bound in Canada.

21 20 19 18 • 4 3 2 1

CONTENTS

*To Layth, Maysa and Zayna with deepest love,
and all my encouragement for the Ramadans to come.*

Indian Muslims break their fast during the month of Ramadan at a mosque in the old part of the city. New Delhi, India.
iStock.com/BDphoto

Chapter Four:
Ramadan Traditions Around the World

Henna decorations on the hand to celebrate Eid.
Athif Ali Khan

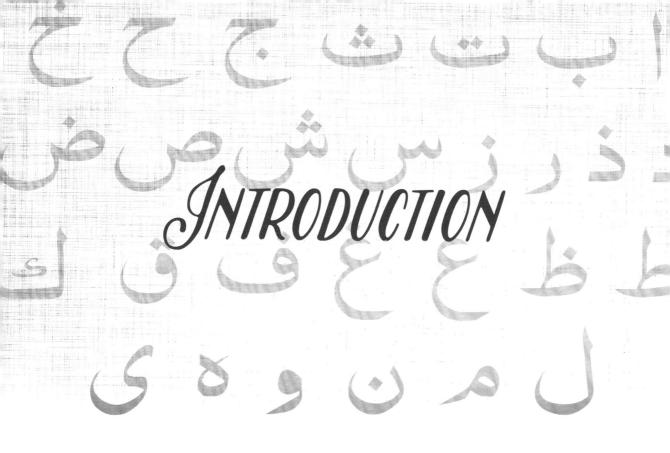

INTRODUCTION

I remember my first *Ramadan* as clearly as if it were yesterday. And by this I mean the first time I kept a fast during Ramadan, the holy month of fasting for **Muslims**. I was 9 years old and I lived in Prince Albert, Saskatchewan, a beautiful city on the prairies with long, hot, very dry summers. The summer of the first Ramadan I fasted, the sun was setting at around 9:30 PM.

When the sun rises or sets is very important to a kid who is fasting. The fast begins at dawn and ends at sunset. So on a typical Ramadan summer day you could begin fasting around four o'clock in the morning and break your fast at nine thirty at night. This means you wouldn't have anything to eat or drink for fifteen hours or

Saskatchewan wheat fields.
iStock.com/4loops

more—which can sound a little like you're a prisoner in a very unpleasant jail cell.

But in my case, I was free. I was freely choosing to fast, and I was so excited to join the grown-ups in observing a tradition that seemed thrillingly mysterious and important. I was going to be part of an exclusive club, and I remember feeling incredibly proud of myself. My older sister was also fasting, and her example inspired me to fast.

Only things didn't go exactly as planned.

My mom woke me up early in the morning, when it was still dark outside. I was bleary-eyed and cranky, but then I remembered I had begged her to wake me up so I wouldn't miss my first fast. She fried homemade donuts and made peanut-butter sandwiches for us to eat with glasses of cold milk. The kitchen was filled with the sweet

Ayesha and Ausma Khan with their mother, Nasima Khan, wearing Eid gharara.

Dr. Zehanat Ali Khan

smell of donuts. I didn't want any milk (just the donuts!), but my mother assured me I would thank her for making me both eat and drink so early in the morning. When we finished our early breakfast, my sister and I brushed our teeth and made the intention to fast, a simple prayer that amounts to saying, "I intend to fast this day in Ramadan."

We stumbled through the morning prayer and fell back into bed.

The next time I woke up, I remembered another reason why the day of my first fast was so important. I'd been looking forward to going over to my friend's house all week. Sara lived on the other side of the city and our parents were also friends, so our two families had planned to spend the day together.

What I forgot was that my friend was Hindu, not Muslim, so she wouldn't be observing Ramadan with me. She'd planned for us to spend the afternoon at the park near her house. This was a special treat because the park had a huge jungle gym, a merry-go-round, loads of swings and a splash pad.

I was still very full from my donut and peanut butter breakfast, so it was easy for me to join in the fun. We ran around the park for hours—swinging, climbing, chasing each other, playing tag. But a few hours later, it hit me.

The sun was beating down on my head. I was boiling hot, and I felt exhausted. Sara and I flopped down on the grass just as an ice-cream cart rolled by. Sara offered to buy me an orange Popsicle, my favorite flavor. Right away, I said yes. Then I remembered my fast and regretfully changed my mind. There was a golden retriever lolling on the grass in front of us, his pink tongue hanging out of his mouth. He was panting in the heat, which was exactly

Some people may get dehydrated when fasting, or experience headaches or increased stress. For Muslims who fast during Ramadan, it's important to drink plenty of fluids during **suhoor** and **iftar**. Doctors don't recommend fasting for people who suffer from eating disorders or as a solution for weight loss in general.

Healthy iftar snacks at a Ramadan iftar party.

Noor Shaikh

what I felt like doing—panting. But I couldn't break my fast in front of anyone.

I told Sara I had to use the washroom, so I ran back to her house while she waited.

All the parents were in the backyard, so no one knew I had come back to the house. I made sure no one was looking, and then I poured myself a glass of cold water from the tap. It was so good that I immediately drank a second one. Then I washed the glass and hid it away and ran all the way back to the park.

I had just done something terrible. I had intentionally broken my fast because I couldn't keep it any longer. I had been fasting for about eight hours and that was as long as I could last. Of course, I didn't eat anything or drink again until sunset. Those two glasses of water had transformed me—first with energy, then with a heavy load of guilt.

It would have been so much better if I'd just waited to fast instead of making a promise I couldn't keep. But I was

9 years old, so it didn't take me long to throw myself back into the excitement of playing with Sara at the park.

I broke fast with everyone else that night and accepted everyone's praise and good wishes with a wide smile and happy self-congratulations, as if I'd actually kept my fast. I was feeling pretty good until I was alone in my room at night. Then the guilt really hit me. I'd begun the most important religious tradition my family observed with a half-truth—all for a glass of water. I've learned a lot of lessons since then, including the purpose behind the month of fasting. The holy month of Ramadan isn't meant to be a punishment: Muslims see it as a blessing.

I know now there would have been no harm in confessing the truth, or admitting I didn't feel well or waiting until I was older to fast. No one would have been angry with me or disappointed. They would have encouraged me to try again.

This is the first time I've told the story of the 9-year-old who couldn't keep her fast. The secret is out at last!

To give you a sense of what Muslim kids think about fasting for a whole month, I asked a few of them to tell me what Ramadan means to them. You'll find their answers in each chapter of this book.

Fig and date cookies on Eid morning.
Summer Shaikh

Sweets on Eid morning, savaiyaan and mitai are traditional Pakistani Eid offerings
Summer Shaikh

"Ramadan is a humbling experience that allows us to empathize with others and reminds us to be thankful for the life we live, and to go on living with an open mind, with love in our hearts and peace emanating from within."
—Zahra, age 17

11

Al-Masjid Al-Ḥarām, in Mecca, Hejaz, Saudi Arabia.

ONE

WHAT IS RAMADAN?

What Is Islam and Who Is a Muslim?

Islam is a *monotheistic* tradition, a religion with more than 1.6 billion followers worldwide. A ***monotheistic religion*** is one that holds that there is only one god, rather than many different gods. Historically, Islam came after Judaism and Christianity. It arrived in the Arabian peninsula in 610 CE (Common Era). Today that part of the world is known as Saudi Arabia. Two of the holiest sites in Islam, the cities of **Mecca** and **Medina**, are located in Saudi Arabia.

Muslims are followers of Islam, who worship the same God as Jews and Christians but call God the Arabic name **Allah**. Muslims also recognize and respect the same

Mecca is considered a holy city of Islam because it's where the messenger of Islam, the Prophet Muhammad, was born. At the cave of **Hira** outside Mecca, the message of the **Qur'an** was transmitted to the Prophet Muhammad through the Angel Gabriel.

prophets found in the Torah and the Bible, including Abraham, Noah, Isaac, Ishmael, Job, John, David, Solomon, Moses, Aaron and Jesus. Mary, the mother of Jesus, is mentioned thirty-four times in the holy book of Muslims, which is called the Qur'an (or **Koran**). A chapter of the Qur'an is named after the Virgin Mary and describes the birth of Jesus. The prophets Abraham, Moses and Jesus are very important figures in the Qur'an. Muslims, Christians and Jews share a tradition that worships one God and urges its followers to live lives full of mercy, goodness and justice.

The word *Islam* has two meanings: submission and peace. One who submits to or accepts Islam's message is a Muslim. Muslims believe the message of Islam was

View above the cave of Hira.
Shutterstock.com/Nufa Qaiesz

delivered by the Angel Gabriel through the recitation of verses of the Qur'an to a man named **Muhammad** at a cave called Hira.

Muhammad is known as the prophet or messenger of God. He was born in the city of Mecca in Arabia in 570 CE. He would often travel to the cave of Hira to think about his purpose in life, and to reflect on where humanity came from, and where people end up after they die. When he was 40 years old, he began to hear the voice of someone he couldn't see, which he found frightening. But he was reassured by the Angel Gabriel that God had chosen him as a messenger for his people. Muhammad received the divine revelation of the Qur'an over a period that lasted twenty-two years.

The Five Pillars of Islam

Muslims believe that the religion of Islam consists of five pillars:

1. **Shahadah**: The act of bearing witness to the Oneness of God
2. **Salah**: Prayer—Muslims pray five times a day
3. **Zakah**: Charity—Giving to charity every year
4. **Sawm**: Fasting—to fast during the holy month of Ramadan
5. **Hajj**: Pilgrimage—performing a pilgrimage to Mecca

Fasting in Ramadan: A Pillar of Islam

One of the pillars of Islam is to fast during the holy month of Ramadan. Fasting is another means of submitting

Ramadan Facts

The Qur'an Competition

Every year, over a two-week period in Ramadan, dozens of Muslim children from around the world go to Cairo, Egypt, to participate in the International Holy Koran Competition. The kids can be as young as 7 years old.

What does it mean to participate? During the competition rounds, the participants showcase their skills at reciting passages of the Qur'an they've learned by heart. Some of the kids have memorized the entire Qur'an. Someone who has memorized the whole Qur'an is known as a **Hafiz** (male) or **Hafiza** (female). What makes the contest especially interesting is that many of the children who compete are not from Arabic-speaking backgrounds. Yet they've become fluent reciting the Qur'an in a language they don't speak and often don't understand!

A documentary film titled *Koran by Heart* traces the journey of three 10-year-old competitors (one girl and two boys) from Senegal, Tajikistan and the Maldives. These kids represent their families, countries and culture by memorizing the Qur'an and participating in the contest.

15

Muslim boys prostrate in prayer.
iStock.com/DistinctiveImages

> "Ramadan means that I get to be reborn spiritually. It's almost like my whole self has been cleansed."
> —Dena, age 15

to God, and Muslims consider fasting an important part of their worship. The month of Ramadan is an opportunity to learn some key lessons. Here are some of the important benefits of fasting:

- Becoming recharged in all areas of your life
- Feeling empathy for those who are less fortunate
- Strengthening a sense of community
- Reaffirming the belief that all human beings are equal

The month of Ramadan offers the opportunity to become closer to God and to improve one's personal and spiritual behavior. By focusing on positive thoughts and actions, Muslims build a closer connection with God and come away from the month feeling spiritually renewed.

Fasting teaches Muslims empathy; feeling the pangs of hunger and thirst all day, as I did when I was a 9-year-old, teaches us to empathize with others who suffer from hunger and thirst. We become more grateful for blessings we usually take for granted, and we understand that it's important and necessary to help others.

Despite the difficulty of fasting for a whole month, Ramadan is a time of great excitement for Muslim families. Though fasting is mandatory only for adults, children look forward to participating in family and community rituals. Families visit the *mosque*, or masjid, more often, and Muslims feel connected to Muslims in other parts of the world, who are also fasting.

When you are hungry and thirsty and tired, you realize that the impact of fasting is the same for everyone who fasts; this emphasizes the fact that as human beings we are all the same, and that no single person is more important than any other. We are equal in the sight of God, and we all struggle, fail and try again, encouraged by what we're trying to accomplish with the fast.

Empathy is the ability to understand and share the feelings of another person, which is different from sympathy, which is feeling compassion for someone else. Empathy is like putting yourself in someone else's shoes.

Muslim girls study their faith.
iStock.com/Yamtono_Sardi

A lunar calendar may have been discovered in the prehistoric caves at Lascaux, France. Dr. Michael Rappenglueck of the University of Munich believes that the cave paintings at Lascaux record the various phases of the moon. If this is true, a 15,000-year-old lunar calendar has been found.

Sunset signals the end of the fast.
Shutterstock.com/sabirmallick

The Ninth Month of the Islamic Lunar Calendar

Ramadan is the ninth month of the Islamic calendar, which is a **lunar calendar**. Because the lunar calendar is a little different from the 365-day **solar calendar** that people normally use, the month of Ramadan falls at a different time each year. A lunar month refers to the time it takes for the moon to orbit Earth, which is approximately twenty-nine and a half days. A lunar month often ends up being shorter than a solar month by a day, which translates into a lunar year being anywhere from ten to twelve days shorter than a solar year. This means that the month of Ramadan comes eleven days earlier in the solar year than the year before. It also means that in some years the month of Ramadan is twenty-nine days long,

while in other years it's thirty days. When Ramadan falls during a hot, dry spell, you're really praying for a shorter lunar month!

Eid prayer at the Taj Mahal, Agra, India.
iStock.com

The sighting of a new moon signals both the beginning and the end of the month of Ramadan. At the end of Ramadan, when a new moon is sighted—either by the naked eye or by astronomical calculations, or by a combination of both—the month of fasting is over, and the time of celebration begins. A new moon at the end of Ramadan signals the beginning of the festival of *Eid-al-Fitr*.

The Month of the Qur'an

Muslims believe the first verses of the Qur'an were revealed to the Prophet Muhammad at the cave of Hira on the twenty-seventh night of Ramadan. When Muslims pray, they recite verses of the Qur'an during their prayers.

19

Ramadan prayers.
iStock.com/501212045

The month of the Ramadan is the month when the first Qur'anic revelation took place. During Ramadan, routine acts in the lives of Muslims have extra value and meaning, so Muslims make the effort to read and understand the Qur'an with fresh eyes in Ramadan, and to commit to its teachings all over again.

Some Muslims believe that all Muslims should perform special evening prayers during the entire month of Ramadan, in addition to the five daily prayers. These special prayers are called **Taraweeh prayers**, and if Muslims go to the mosque for Taraweeh prayers, the **Imam**, who is the leader of the congregation, will recite the entire Qur'an, a section at a time. Toward the end of the month of Ramadan, usually a few days before the month ends, the entire Qur'an will have been completed—an occasion for great celebration. Sometimes you feel a bit sleepy during those long Taraweeh prayers—but the light at the end of the tunnel is the light at the end of the Qur'an.

Muslims read much more of the Qur'an during the month of Ramadan than at any other time of year. It allows for greater knowledge of our faith and greater commitment to the values of justice and equality taught by the Qur'an. I learned to read the formal Arabic of the Qur'an when I was a child but, like many Muslims who are not from an Arabic-speaking background, I never understood it, except for some important words that occur frequently, like *salah*, *zakah* and *Ramadan*. Nowadays I make a point of also reading the English translation, so I can better understand the message of the Qur'an.

"Ramadan is spiritual, it's relaxing, but Ramadan is also tiring."
—*Bilal, age 18*

A Muslim boy meditates on the Qur'an.
iStock.com/BERKO85

Ramadan Facts

Health Benefits and Concerns

An article in the scientific journal *Cell Stem Cell* discussed some of the health benefits of fasting. In an experiment conducted with mice, the mice that fasted for two to four days over a period of six months began to generate new immune cells to replace old and damaged ones. The team that carried out the experiment learned that if cancer patients fasted for three days before the cancer treatment of chemotherapy, they were more likely to be protected against the damage to their immune systems that chemotherapy often causes. Other studies have shown that people who fast now and then may see improvement in their blood pressure and cholesterol levels. This type of intermittent fasting may reduce the risk of getting diabetes, though further scientific study is required in all these areas.

The Requirements of Fasting

Suhoor

The daily fast during the month of Ramadan begins at dawn. Muslims make an early breakfast. During my teenage years I wasn't much of a cook, so I used to rely on my mother's excellent cooking. My siblings and I would enjoy a hearty breakfast of *rotis* (a thin, round Pakistani bread) and omelets or kebabs. This pre-fast meal is called suhoor in Arabic. Before eating, I would make the intention to fast. After finishing breakfast, I'd brush my teeth and wash up for the morning prayer, **Fajr**. Then I'd fall back into bed.

Prayer

When my siblings and I were kids, we were lazy about performing our prayers. My mother used to warn us that

A Muslim student learns to read the Qur'an.
iStock.com/seksanwangjaisuk

Asking for blessings at the end of prayer.
iStock.com/Reddiplomat

if we couldn't be bothered to pray, we shouldn't bother fasting—one was no good without the other. I still struggle with performing my prayers on a regular basis, but because of my mother's warnings, the month of Ramadan is the one time of year that, no matter what I'm doing, I'll make sure I get to those prayers on time. Otherwise I'm left with the sense that I missed the real purpose of the fast: it wasn't to deny myself food and drink but to engage in a spiritual commitment. My mom's fear tactics worked!

Apart from praying, Muslims carry on with their daily activities during Ramadan—though every now and again they may find themselves snatching a nap or limiting their participation in sports. But the point of fasting isn't to spend the day asleep—it's to engage in productive work and to focus on your personal conduct while increasing

"It's less about feeding our physical bodies and more about feeding our spiritual bodies. We focus on worship and purify and replenish our faith."
—Humza, age 16

23

Famlies gather in Sultanahmet square in Istanbul, Turkey for an Iftar picnic.

iStock.com/franz12

your capacity to be generous and kind. This takes work, especially when you have a raging headache. But as you get used to the rhythms of fasting, some of the difficulty begins to ease and your body learns to handle it. Recent scientific studies have shown that short-term fasting has important physical benefits.

Iftar

When the sun sets, it's time to break the fast. In Arabic, this time is called iftar. It's common for Muslim families to host dinner parties for iftar, so that people can break their fast together and pray as a community. My entire life has been filled with one iftar party after another, and it's one of the reasons I most look forward to Ramadan. Because I'm from a Pakistani background, my family breaks fast in three steps. First we break our fast by reciting a short prayer and eating a date. We eat dates as a way of following the tradition of the Prophet Muhammad, who used to open his fast with dates and encouraged his followers to do the same. Next we set up a table of light snacks; for my family that means *samosas*, *pakoras*, two or three kinds of chutney, fruit sliced and spiced up as fruit *chaat*, and cold glasses of a buttermilk-infused drink called *lassi*. After this quick snack, everyone rushes to wash up and pray the short dusk prayer called **Maghrib**. Then comes the real meal. For a month that is all about fasting, Muslim families spend a great deal of time shopping for food and preparing food to break the fast—maybe too much time. After you've been fasting all day, it's tempting to stuff yourself at night, but that would undo the purpose of the fast, which is to learn self-discipline and gratitude, among other things.

A traditional Pakistani Eid lunch
Summer Shaikh

When making this recipe as well as the other recipes in this book, be sure an adult is around to supervise.

Homemade Lassi

Lassi is a cold, refreshing drink served at iftar time and can be made with either yogurt or buttermilk. It can be a salty preparation or a sweet one flavored with frozen or fresh fruit. This simple variation is my favorite and is always best served with ice cubes.

Ingredients:

1 quart buttermilk

6 eight-ounce glasses ice-cold water

¼ cup sugar

Directions:

1. Mix the ingredients in a jug and add more sugar if needed. Refrigerate and serve at iftar.

Variation: Add 1 teaspoon salt and ½ teaspoon cardamom seeds for flavor.

The city of Medina is where the Prophet Muhammad sought refuge from persecution by the people of Mecca. The people who received Muhammad in Medina are known as the **Ansar**, or "the Helpers." Medina is also the city where the Prophet Muhammad died.

Muslim girl offers a warm greeting.
Dreamstime.com/DiversityStudio1

Exceptions: Valid Reasons Not to Fast

Because fasting is challenging, it's natural to ask whether every single Muslim has to fast during the month of Ramadan. Fasting is a form of devotion done out of a deep love for God. It's meant to increase closeness to God, not as a punishment, so there are reasonable exceptions to fasting. Every sane, able, adult Muslim is required to fast during the month of Ramadan, but the following people are *not* required to fast: children, the elderly, pregnant and nursing women, women who are menstruating, those who aren't mentally fit, and those who are enduring great hardship, such as from war, disease, famine, illness or long and difficult travel.

In each case, Muslims who wish to fast may do so, and those who are unable to fast may make up the fasts when they are able to. My mother, who has always been my inspiration, is quite capable of fasting for several months in a row. I, on the other hand, greet the end of Ramadan like a shipwrecked sailor flagging down a rescue vessel—until the next year, when I begin the month of fasting all over again.

Uzma's Story

When Uzma was young her parents didn't let her eat takeout food very often because of the difficulty of finding **halal** food. (*Halal* is the Arabic word for "allowed" or "permissible." Halal food is prepared in accordance with Muslim dietary laws.) When Uzma did go out to eat it was mainly for seafood, and her favorite meal was the fish sandwich at a local burger chain. The very first fast she kept, she missed waking up for the pre-fast meal. She decided to fast anyway, though her parents strongly discouraged her. When her parents realized she was determined to fast, they invited their family and friends over to celebrate. To encourage her, they told her she could have whatever she wanted to eat that night. Uzma was obsessed with the fish sandwich, so that's what she asked for. Knowing she'd get what she asked for at the end of the day helped Uzma make it through her fast. Uzma's parents also bought a fish sandwich for everyone who joined them. Twenty-five fish sandwiches drenched in salt and grease made up that night's Ramadan dinner. When asked about it today, Uzma says, "I will never forget the image of my childhood home filled with biryani-loving immigrants, all making faces, as they had to break their fasts with that sandwich!"

Uzma is dressed up for Eid.
Uzma

Ibtihaj's Story

American Olympian Ibtihaj Muhammad.
Shutterstock.com/Leonard Zhukovsky

Ibtihaj Muhammad is an American Muslim and an Olympic fencer. Olympic athletes must train long hours in their sport over a period of many years. Ibtihaj has said that she normally trains up to seven hours a day but that her schedule has to change during the month of Ramadan. She still needs to train and compete at an elite level, but she organizes her day a little differently when she's fasting. Normally Ibtihaj trains for two hours in the morning and another five in the late afternoon to evening. But when she's fasting she begins her rigorous physical routine earlier in the day, so she's finished her fencing workouts much earlier in the afternoon. And her diet changes to include more superfoods and protein when she's fasting. Because she's been doing this for so long, Ibtihaj knows how to take care of her body while she's training and fasting.

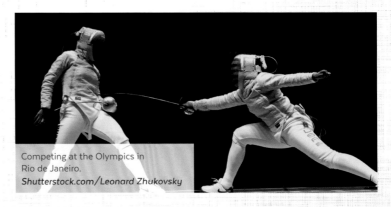

Competing at the Olympics in Rio de Janeiro.
Shutterstock.com/Leonard Zhukovsky

Ibtihaj Muhammad in fine fencing form.

TWO

THE STAGES OF RAMADAN

The Three Ashras

Ramadan is a chance for Muslims to start fresh and wipe their slates clean by asking God for mercy, showing mercy to others, and working toward a peaceful reward in the afterlife.

Many Muslims believe that the month of Ramadan is divided into three parts, each of which is called an **ashra**, or ten-day period. The Prophet Muhammad once said, "The first part of Ramadan is for mercy, the middle for forgiveness, and the third part for salvation."

The first ten days, or first Ashra, of Ramadan is for mercy. This is a time when Muslims reflect on their conduct. Have they acted in good faith? Have they been honest, reliable, thoughtful, generous and kind? Have they

Lanterns.
iStock.com/pictafolio

Children in Dhaka, Bangladesh.
iStock.com/Melih Cevdet Teksen

"Ramadan is a time to remember God and to get closer to your community."
—Nadia, age 14

been courteous to others? Have they atoned for all kinds of bad behavior: lies, deceit, small trickeries or other forms of dishonesty? Have they asked forgiveness for committing acts that are forbidden to Muslims, such as stealing or harming others? Muslims believe that in the first ten days of Ramadan, God's mercy exists in abundance. When a person is ready to change their bad habits, these ten days are full of God's mercy.

The second Ashra is for forgiveness. During these ten days, just as Muslims seek God's mercy for their own transgressions, they must demonstrate that they are serious about it by showing mercy to others. Suppose you had a fight with a friend. Or you gossiped about someone behind their back. Or someone insulted you for no reason, and your immediate instinct was to insult them in return. The second Ashra of Ramadan is the perfect time to demonstrate your capacity for forgiveness. A Christian might call this "turning the other cheek." You apologize to others for your misdeeds, and you accept the desire of others to be forgiven in turn. Muslims swiftly learn that forgiveness takes hard work and a generous spirit—but if they want to be forgiven for their own misdeeds, they must practice by demonstrating forgiveness themselves.

The third Ashra sounds dire. Some translations from Arabic describe the last ten days of Ramadan as the period for emancipation, or being freed, from hellfire. Other translators call this period "deliverance," or being rescued. I like the term *salvation*. Just as Hindus and Buddhists meditate, Muslims pray. Muslims believe the last ten days of Ramadan offer them an opportunity for their souls to reach a beautiful final destination—a salvation or deliverance from the punishment of hellfire.

This third Ashra of Ramadan encourages prayer, good deeds and self-reflection. The Day of Judgment or Accounting promises Muslims a just rendering of all they accomplished during their lives. Did you live a good life? Were you kind and just to others? You will face a fair accounting for that. But were you cruel and unjust? You will also face an accounting for that.

Some Muslims are fearful of the idea of hellfire. But most Muslims understand that a well-lived life is its own reward, and it's one that ensures a peaceful afterlife—or, as the Qur'an promises, "gardens through which rivers flow."

Like Christians and Jews, Muslims believe God is the most just of all judges and that not a single one of their deeds is measured out of balance. Personally, that makes me feel hopeful, even though in many parts of the world Muslim communities are suffering from persecution,

Ramadan Facts

The Night of Destiny

We have sent it down (the Qur'an) on the Night of Destiny.

And do you know what the Night of Destiny is?

The Night of Destiny is better than a thousand months.

Angels descend in hosts by the leave of their Lord to carry out every command.

It is peaceful until the coming of Dawn.

—Sura Al-Qadr (The Night of Destiny, Chapter 97:1–5 of the Qur'an)

Praying inside Suleymaniye Mosque in Istanbul, Turkey.
iStock.com/EnginKorkmaz

poverty and war. Observing Ramadan in Syria, for example, is particularly difficult, as many parts of the country are under siege, and food supplies and clean water are scarce to begin with. In Yemen and South Sudan a famine is taking place, and it is nearly impossible to fast for a month. The dire conditions in many parts of the Muslim world are another reason for Muslims to empathize with their fellow human beings during this holy month and to do their best to bring about positive change to ease the suffering of others.

The Mysterious Night of Destiny

A magical event occurs during the last ten nights of Ramadan. Tradition holds that one of the last odd-numbered nights of Ramadan (the twenty-first, the

Prophet Muhammad's saying describes how central charity is to faith: Every act of goodness is charity.

—*Sahih Muslim's Book of Prophet Muhammad's Sayings, Hadith #496*

Syrian Refugee children in one of the tented camps in Beqaa, Lebanon.

iStock.com/AhmadSabra

Cave of Hira.
Shutterstock.com/artpixelgraphy Studi

twenty-third, the twenty-fifth and so on) is a blessed and holy night known as the **Night of Power** or the **Night of Destiny**. For Muslims, it is the holiest night of the year.

Many Muslims believe that the twenty-seventh night of Ramadan is the Night of Destiny. Others say that it's impossible to know with certainty which of the last ten nights is this special night, so they observe *all* the odd-numbered nights as a possible Night of Destiny.

But what is the Night of Destiny?

Revelation first came to Muhammad, the messenger of God, on the Night of Destiny, in a small cave called Hira. **Laylat-al-Qadr** commemorates the night the Qur'an was first revealed to Muhammad. The first words of the Qur'an urge Muhammad to "Read! In the Name of Your Lord, Who created humankind from an embryo."

In Arabic, the Night of Power, or the Night of Destiny, is called Laylat-al-Qadr. In Persian, or Farsi, a language spoken in Iran, and in Urdu, a language spoken in Pakistan, the Night of Destiny is called Shub-e-Qadr.

Ramadan Facts

A Christmas Story

When I was in fourth grade, I lived in Prince Albert, Saskatchewan, where I went to John Diefenbaker Public School. Every year our school would have a Christmas pageant. My sister and I were the only Muslim kids in the school at the time. I knew we didn't celebrate Christmas, but I wasn't too clear on why. I badly wanted to be part of the pageant, so I asked my mom what I could do to join in. My classmates were representing Christmas traditions from around the world, and for some reason I really wanted to be the kid who wished everyone "*Feliz Navidad*" because it sounded so beautiful. My mom suggested that my sister and I dress up in our fancy Eid outfits and wish everyone "**Eid Mubarak**" instead. Because my parents are from Pakistan, my mom made us beautiful dresses called *ghararas*. They were pink and looked a little like patchwork quilts. We wore them with short tops and long chiffon veils, and we paraded down the stage calling out "Eid Mubarak" with gusto.

Eid-al-Fitr and Christmas represent completely different occasions, but they inspire the same feelings of joy and celebration in the communities that observe them. I felt like I really belonged at my school's Christmas pageant that night.

Young people in Nigeria.
iStock.com/peeterv

Because the Night of Destiny is such a sacred night, many Muslims will stay awake and pray through the night, asking for blessings and forgiveness and spiritual strength. For those who are ill or grieving or suffering any kind of burden or hardship, the Night of Destiny offers comfort and hope. Chapter 97 of the Qur'an is named "The Night of Destiny."

I love the idea of angels among us, though I have no idea what form they may take—or whether they're real or just symbolic, standing for something else. The Night of Destiny and the time of fast-breaking are so special to Muslims that we feel the presence of angels all around us. When we break our fasts we say a special prayer. My brothers and sister and I used to tease one other about the angels: if one of us took more than our fair share of dessert, we'd joke that the angels had seen him or her do it and were sending a report to the Great Upstairs. When my nephews and nieces were very small, I told them they never needed to worry because they always had angels watching over them on their shoulders. As soon as I told one of my nieces this, she playfully smacked both her shoulders!

It may seem like we weren't taking the idea of these messengers seriously, but actually it shows how comfortable we were with the idea that angels are all around us—they're part of our lives, keeping an eye on things, so to speak.

> "What Ramadan means to me is that it's a chance to grow. I call it a month of self-discipline."
> —*Layth, age 13*

Eid-al-Fitr: The Great Celebration

After a month of fasting and long nights of prayer, Muslims are ready for a celebration. Eid-al-Fitr arrives at the end of Ramadan and is decided by the sighting of

After morning prayers at the Jama Masjid in New Delhi on the occasion of Eid-al-Fitr.
iStock.com/sauvik

the new moon. Eid-al-Fitr is the Festival of Breaking the Fast. On the last night of Ramadan, no Taraweeh prayers are observed. The next morning, Muslims dress up in their nicest clothes and attend the congregational prayer, which is different from all the other prayers that Muslims offer. The Eid prayer, or salah, is offered before noon on Eid morning.

The Eid salah is usually held in an open area such as a field if the weather is nice, or in a great hall or a mosque. One year I attended Eid salah at the SkyDome (now Rogers Centre) in Toronto. This was an especially memorable occasion because I was able to see thousands of Muslims coming together to pray: black, white, brown—people of all cultural backgrounds and traditions. Everyone was smiling and hugging one another. After the prayer the Muslim community had organized crafts and games for

The Eid prayer consists of two rak'ahs, or cycles of prayer, and includes twelve special takbirs, or greetings to God. The takbir "Allahu Akbar" means "God is greatest."

Girl at a market at Nizwa, Oman, on Eid-al-Fitr
Shutterstock.com/Katiekk

the kids, and there were plenty of stalls where snacks were sold as well. We enjoyed this part of the day enormously, before rushing home for more festivities.

In addition to all the fun, the Eid prayer consists of a sermon called the **khutbah**. One of the most important sermons ever given was the last sermon by the Prophet Muhammad, near the end of his life. During this sermon he emphasized the pillars of Islam and encouraged the community of believers to treat one another with kindness, mercy and justice. He added an extremely important lesson about the equality of human beings when he said, "Remember, one day you will appear before God to answer for your deeds. So beware, do not stray from the path of righteousness after I am gone. All mankind is from Adam and Eve, an Arab has no superiority over a non-Arab, nor does a non-Arab have any superiority over an Arab. A white person has no superiority over a black person, nor does a black person have any superiority over a white person except by piety and the doing of good deeds." He also emphasized the importance of fasting during the month of Ramadan in his final sermon.

Muslims hear a regular sermon once a week at Friday prayer, but the Eid sermon is delivered only on Eid. An imam will reflect on the lessons of the month of Ramadan that has just passed, and he will encourage Muslims to keep up good practices for the rest of the year as well. The khutbah encourages us to be kind, forgiving and generous all year long—and not to save all our good behavior for the month of Ramadan. One of my favorite imams used to joke that there are three types of Muslims: Abdullah, who is a Muslim all year long, Abdul Ramadan, who remembers

"Ramadan is the holy month in which all Muslims are called to abstain from eating and drinking during the daylight hours. This lets us reflect on our spirituality. We go to the mosque, donate to charity or read Qur'an. We try to fulfill the pillars of Islam."
—*Layla, age 14*

Gathering for a communal charity iftar in Sultanahmet Park in Istanbul, Turkey.
Shutterstock.com/isa_ozdere

he's a Muslim during the month of Ramadan, and Abdul Eid, who remembers he's a Muslim only on Eid day. The point of community is to welcome every type of Muslim and to encourage others in their practice, all year long.

Eid Charity

On Eid day it's also important to remember charity. Every adult Muslim must make a small donation that day for themselves and their dependents, according to their means. This type of charity is called **zakat-al-fitr**, after Eid-al-Fitr. Most Muslims will give zakat-al-fitr at the mosque on Eid day.

But there is a much more important form of charity called zakah, which all Muslims must give if they are able. Muslims with the financial means to do so must give a part of their savings to charity each year. This form of giving should always be donated to those in need or to projects that assist the poor: for example, you could give your zakah to a clean water project in Pakistan or South Sudan, or you could donate it to a home-building project for people in your community who are homeless. Where you donate your zakah is up to you: many Muslim families give it to poorer members of their extended families or to local schools. Some families prefer to give their zakah during Ramadan to practice the values of Ramadan.

A third type of charity is called **sadaqa**. Sadaqa is a voluntary form of giving that Muslims may participate in at any time of year, including during Ramadan. Sadaqa can refer to any act of kindness, generosity or friendship. It can be a service you perform to help others or money you donate to people in need or other worthy causes.

Ramadan Facts

Eidy

In my house Eid is the happiest and most important day of the year. We dress up in our nicest clothes, we go to the mosque for prayer and then we come home to be with family and friends. For all the years I lived with my parents and three siblings, we hosted a huge party at our house on Eid day. We would clean the house from top to bottom and spend the whole week before Eid cooking. Then we would entertain friends and serve food throughout the day. By the end of the night, we could barely move.

Another thing I fondly remember is all the adults in the community giving us kids a little bit of money on Eid day. We called this "Eidy." Now that I'm older, no one gives me Eidy anymore. I have twelve nieces and nephews, so by the time Eid is over my funds are seriously depleted!

Although it isn't a must to give money to children on Eid day, it's one of the happy traditions that have evolved along with the holiday, just like girls decorating their hands with henna the night before, or children making Eid decorations for the house, or families hanging decorative lights for Eid.

For example, you could donate to the World Wildlife Fund, or you could help refugees settle in their new homes by donating items they might need for their families.

Muslim families give sadaqa regularly. In my family, every time a member of the family has a piece of good news—such as one of my nieces or nephews doing well in school, or someone getting a new job or getting married—we always donate sadaqa in gratitude. When any member of the family is suffering a setback or difficulty of some kind, such as poor health or a personal loss, we also give or perform some act of sadaqa. Acts of service for the benefit of others are an essential part of the Islamic faith. During the month of Ramadan, Muslims give even more sadaqa than at other times of the year.

> "It doesn't matter what the color of your skin is, what language you speak, or what religion you believe in. We should all consider each other as human beings. We should respect each other and we should all fight for our rights, for the rights of children, the rights of women, and for the rights of every human being."
> —Malala Yousafzai, Winner of the Nobel Peace Prize

MANGO PINEAPPLE SMOOTHIE

A refreshing drink on Eid morning.

When making this recipe as well as the other recipes in this book, be sure an adult is around to supervise.

Ingredients:

1 fresh mango (or the same volume of frozen mango)

1 frozen banana

½ cup almond milk (for people with nut allergies, substitute regular milk)

½ cup sliced or diced pineapple, drained of juice

4 tablespoons plain yogurt

1 tablespoon agave nectar or maple syrup

Directions:

Blend ingredients together in blender and serve chilled.

Hacıveyiszade Mosque.

Hamzah's Story

Hamzah was 12 years old last Ramadan. He went with his parents to the mosque for Friday prayer. During Ramadan he also went for the evening prayers but usually fell asleep. Hamzah was competing with his friend Ali to see who could stay awake the longest. Hamzah and Ali began to play pranks on each other. They stood in the back row to avoid distracting the others (but also so they wouldn't get caught). On the last night of prayer everyone was thrilled to have finished reciting the Qur'an and to have reached the last fast. Hamzah could see that Ali was asleep on his feet. He took a toy horn he'd bought at a novelty store and blew it in Ali's ear. The horn was much louder than he expected—Ali cried out in shock, disrupting the whole prayer.

When Hamzah's father scolded him, Hamzah came up with a quick explanation. He said, "I just wanted to celebrate the last time Ali and I will have to show up for Taraweeh prayers!"

"When you fast, God is showing you how people who don't have food feel. Also, it shows us we are fortunate and should be grateful."
—*Saif, age 11*

A community iftar in Sultanahmet Park in front of the Hagia Sophia in Istanbul, Turkey. Many community Iftar dinners are held in Turkey during Ramadan.

Shutterstock.com/Orlok

THREE

THE SPIRIT OF RAMADAN

Giving Back

Many Muslims treat the month of Ramadan as an opportunity to contribute to their communities through volunteer work. Others make an effort to educate themselves about their heritage as Muslims. Both kinds of efforts are different ways of living the values of Ramadan.

GIVE 30

The GIVE 30 initiative was founded in 2012 by a Canadian Muslim named Ziyaad Mia. Ziyaad wanted to contribute to society in a meaningful way. He was especially concerned about the problem of hunger in many Canadian cities and towns. With the help of family members, friends and

Ziyaad Mia, founder of GIVE 30.

Ziyaad Mia

The Story of the Spider

As the messenger of Islam, Muhammad was persecuted by the citizens of Mecca. He challenged their ideas by calling them to worship one God. The new religion of Islam was seen as a threat by the tribe of the Quraysh—a tribe Muhammad belonged to. He endured persecution as he tried to spread his message. He fled to Medina with one of his closest companions, Abu Bakr.

The Quraysh followed him, intending to kill him. So the prophet and Abu Bakr hid inside a cave at the mountain of Thawr. Afraid for the prophet's life, Abu Bakr asked, "What if they see the two of us hiding in this cave?" Muhammad answered, "What do you think of the fate of we two, Abu Bakr, when God is the third?"

Though the Quraysh searched high and low, they didn't enter the cave because a spider had woven a dazzling web over its entrance. The Quraysh reasoned that no one could have entered the cave because the spider's web was intact. The spider's miraculous web saved the prophet from certain death.

GIVE 30 inspires a community.
Ziyaad Mia

supporters, he launched the GIVE 30 fund-raising campaign to fight against hunger by supporting food banks across Canada. Soon many different cities, such as Winnipeg, Edmonton and Kingston, were participating in GIVE 30 projects, and there is now a GIVE 30 project in New York City.

GIVE 30 proposed a unique idea. Ramadan is a time of year when Muslims voluntarily go without food to develop greater empathy for people in need. To help with the challenges facing those in need, GIVE 30 asked people to donate the money they would normally have spent on food—lunch, snacks or coffee, for example—if they weren't fasting for the month. If Muslims weren't fasting for any reason, GIVE 30 suggested that instead of buying lunch they make their lunch at home and donate the money they would otherwise have spent on lunch to the fight against hunger.

People who participate in the GIVE 30 campaign are acting on an important saying of the Prophet Muhammad: "He is not of us who goes to sleep with a full stomach, while his neighbor remains hungry."

The GIVE 30 food banks campaign is open to everyone—not just Muslims or people who are fasting. The goal is for everyone to work together to build a more compassionate community. GIVE 30 volunteers come from all backgrounds and communities.

During Ramadan 2017 the GIVE 30 campaign raised more than $175,000 to support the efforts of food banks. The organization has raised almost $725,000 since 2012.

"I realized I save a lot of money during Ramadan because I'm not eating. Why not put that money to good use?"
—Ziyaad Mia

Two young boys donate to the GIVE 30 Ramadan campaign.
Ziyaad Mia

Project Downtown

Some years ago, I was the editor of a magazine for Muslim girls in Canada and the United States called *Muslim Girl*. One of the most interesting stories the magazine covered was about a volunteer project called Project Downtown. The story focused on a group of students in Miami, Florida, who founded the program in 2006. Muslim students at the University of Miami were concerned about the problem of homelessness in their city. They began bringing food to homeless people. Within just over a year the students had served more than 10,000 meals.

The young women involved in the program developed a website for donations, arranged food preparation and

Participating members of Project Downtown.
Yaseen Ali

delivery, and coordinated efforts to help combat homeless-ness in other cities. But these young women did more than that. They also took the time to listen. Many of the people they helped wanted to talk about the circumstances that had made them homeless. They wanted to describe what it was like to be homeless, and the members of Project Downtown quickly grew to appreciate the importance of building real relationships to tackle the problems of home-lessness and hunger. Their early work in this area has built many bridges and helped many people.

Today Project Downtown is a student-run commu-nity service organization that works hand in hand with the Muslim Students Association all over the country. Student volunteers participate in Project Downtown programs year-round, but Project Downtown steps up its efforts during the month of Ramadan and runs a

Enriching a community by providing meals during Ramadan.

Yaseen Ali

"We should treat the less fortunate the same way we treat ourselves, and give them the same things we have."

—*Chaman, age 14*

51

Camper participating in an art workshop for teens at a Camp Ramadan in Bethesda, Maryland. *Ayesha Ahmed*

special Ramadan Series. The Ramadan Series emphasizes community-building by providing essential services such as feeding the hungry. Project Downtown runs similar projects in many cities across the United States, as well as in London, England. The students who participate in Project Downtown believe there is no better way to show the spirit of Ramadan than to serve the people of their communities who are most in need.

"We appreciate the things we take for granted, like food and water, and this brings us closer to God."
—*Aniqa, age 15*

Camp Ramadan

Camp Ramadan is a summer day camp founded in 2013 by a group called the Next Wave Muslim Initiative. While many Ramadan programs focus outward on the entire community, Camp Ramadan is a retreat for Muslim children, who often feel the pressure to act as ambassadors for their faith. At Camp Ramadan, Muslim kids are free of that pressure and can focus on fun things like arts and crafts, while also learning about the importance of community service and exploring their diverse cultural heritage.

For example, children from many different backgrounds attend the camp in the Washington, DC, area, but they all learn traditional Islamic arts and crafts, such as calligraphy and bookbinding. Artists teach the kids how to make handmade paper and how to marble it by mixing different paints to produce original works of art. Younger children do crafts such as making spiders or spiderwebs, because of the importance of a spider in the Prophet Muhammad's life. (See "The Story of the Spider" on page 48.)

Many parents and community members volunteer at the camps as part of their community service during Ramadan. Younger campers are asked to collect toys and canned foods to donate to local charities, an activity that

Preparing gifts to give on Eid day.
Athif Ali Khan

Ramadan Facts

The Kindness of Friends and Strangers

It's wonderful to see the kindness of people who don't observe Ramadan during a month when Muslims are fasting. In hospitals and clinics around the country, Muslim doctors and nurses often cover clinics and call schedules for their colleagues on the important holidays of other communities. My youngest brother, Kashif, is a doctor who always takes the Christmas call. Similarly, Muslims receive great consideration and empathy from their colleagues during Ramadan and on Eid al-Fitr; our friends and co-workers often pick up the slack or take extra shifts during Ramadan to help out Muslims who are fasting and staying up late into the night to pray. Or they carry out simple acts of kindness, such as taking food to their neighbors.

Zaib Shaikh, star of the Canadian television show *Little Mosque on the Prairie*, says that a kind member of the Sikh faith had cut his neighbor's lawn instead of his own because his neighbor was fasting for Ramadan. That spirit of consideration is something to be proud of and celebrate.

A young camper is participating in a laser beam challenge at a Camp Ramadan in Bethesda, Maryland. *Ayesha Ahmed*

teaches the campers about the purpose of Ramadan. Older kids participate in workshops about public speaking and team building. Muslim parents are happy that there are some options for the education and entertainment of their children during the long days of fasting.

Though Camp Ramadan is a small, local camp, the demand for these kinds of fun activities for kids has grown quickly. Camp organizers are hoping to be able to serve more and more Muslim communities.

Other Social Programs and Efforts

For many families who rely on food banks, housing takes up more than 70 percent of their income, leaving them hungry and in need. More than 30 percent of the people who depend on food banks are children.

In London, England, the Ramadan Tent Project builds bridges between communities by getting people together to share different points of view. One of its programs, Open Iftar, invites people of all different faiths (or no faith at all) to join together under the Ramadan "tent" to break their fast. The program places a special emphasis on feeding people who are homeless. Open Iftar brings together people from all walks of life to help them get to know about Muslims.

Many other programs, such as Project Ramadan and Project Reach, do similar things: community service, helping people who are hungry and homeless, and answering questions anyone may have about Muslims. Even though Muslims go without food and water during Ramadan, they still the find the energy to practice their values as Muslims.

And in this age of social media, all kinds of new websites now try to make observing Ramadan easier for Muslims. There are websites for listening to the Qur'an and others that discuss the teachings of Islam. There are websites that offer hundreds of Ramadan recipes, and others where Muslims can encourage one another through the hardship of the fast. In the modern age, Ramadan has truly gone global.

"You have to be thankful for the food you have because people around the world don't have as much."
—Maysa, age 12

When making this recipe as well as the other recipes in this book, be sure an adult is around to supervise.

APPLE AND PEAR SALAD
WITH A TWIST OF LEMON

This is a light and refreshing salad that can be served as an appetizer before the main meal at iftar. Prepare an hour before serving.

Ingredients:

2 apples, peeled and cubed
2 pears, peeled and sliced
1 cucumber, peeled and diced
1 can mandarin orange segments
2 tablespoons plain yogurt
1 teaspoon honey
2 teaspoons lemon juice
Handful fresh raspberries
A few fresh mint leaves

Directions:

Mix the ingredients in a large bowl, refrigerate for an hour and serve at iftar time, garnished with raspberries and mint leaves.

An Iftar Story

The first time I was away from home was when I went to law school in Ottawa, Ontario. I didn't know anyone in Ottawa, and when Ramadan came around during the school year I felt really lonely. Ramadan had always been a time of community for me, and I was usually surrounded by dozens of family members and friends. This time I was alone. But I was soon invited to join my school's Muslim Students Association, and with a number of other students I volunteered to organize an iftar for all the Muslim kids at school. The problem was that I didn't know how to cook, and neither did any of the other members. We thought we'd try making spaghetti—for about 100 people! But instead of using spaghetti we bought linguini noodles. After we'd boiled them we forgot to wash them, so by the time we served the dinner, the noodles were stuck together in these huge, sticky balls. It was impossible to get any spaghetti sauce on them.

A hundred people had come to break their fast that night! They'd been hungry all day and were really looking forward to their dinner—but the only dinner to be had was a tray of salad, which even I couldn't ruin. Some kind person ran out and bought loads of samosas for everyone to eat. My friends joked with me that it was a good thing that Ramadan was a time of forgiveness—otherwise I'd be in deep trouble! Needless to say, I wasn't invited to be part of the iftar committee again.

Salima's Story

Salima's family knows all the other families in their neighborhood, Muslim and non-Muslim alike. By the time Salima turned 12, her neighbors knew all about Ramadan's rituals and traditions. Each year Salima made crafts to decorate her house for Ramadan. She hung a glittery star and crescent moon on the outside of her front door. She also baked all kinds of desserts. The week before Ramadan began, Salima made baklava and coconut macaroons. She tied them up with ribbons in colorful gift bags and gave them to her neighbors. Her neighbors used to ask Salima why she was handing out these sweets, but now they know the answer: Salima wanted to share the joy and goodwill of Ramadan. In recent years a few of Salima's friends who aren't Muslim tried fasting just to keep her company. In Salima's neighborhood the whole community enjoys the blessings of Ramadan.

A festive serving of baklava.
Noor Shaikh

Children in Zanzibar, Tanzania.

FOUR

RAMADAN TRADITIONS AROUND THE WORLD

Often you will see the terms "Muslim world" or "Islamic world," but they can be misleading. Around 23 percent of the world's population is Muslim, and in forty-nine different countries Muslims are the majority of citizens. These countries have their own cultures, customs and languages. Though Muslims share a common faith, their cultural and religious practices are quite diverse, so there really is no such thing as a single "Muslim world" or "Islamic world."

Muslim women in Sarajevo, Bosnia, at the Mosque of Gazi Husrev-beg.
Shutterstock.com/Petr Bonek

Bosnia

In Bosnia, Ramadan has knit itself into the fabric of the nation. Vacations are often organized around this month, work days are shorter than usual, and two official

Ramadan Facts

The Dissolution of Yugoslavia

There used to be a country named Yugoslavia in Eastern Europe, but in 1990 Yugoslavia began to dissolve into separate republics. The republic of Slovenia *seceded* from (left) Yugoslavia in 1990, and the republic of Croatia seceded in 1991. Both republics came under attack by the Yugoslav National Army. In 1992 the republic of Bosnia and Herzegovina declared independence from Yugoslavia. The war in Bosnia began with the bombing of the capital city, Sarajevo, in 1992 and reached its most tragic moment with the Srebrenica massacre in 1995, when 8,000 Muslim men and boys were killed. During the war 100,000 people were killed. They came from many different backgrounds and groups, but the majority of the war's victims were Bosnian Muslims who were targeted *because* they were Muslim. The International Criminal Tribunal for the former Yugoslavia has since recognized that *genocide* was committed in Bosnia.

Young women at the Mosque of Gazi Husrev-beg in Sarajevo, Bosnia.
Shutterstock.com/Petr Bonek

holidays are given for Eid-al-Fitr. To celebrate Eid, shops and streets are strung with lights. Mosques fill up during Ramadan, and Muslims prepare special foods for morning and evening meals. Bosnian Muslims think of fasting as an individual effort and the festival of Eid-al-Fitr as a communal celebration. However, the celebration has a sad side as well. Because of the war in Bosnia that lasted from 1992 to 1995, Bosnia's **Grand Mufti**, or religious leader, declared the second day of Eid a day to remember people who died during the war.

China

There are twenty-four million Muslims and thousands of mosques in China. Two of China's mosques are famous: the Niujie Mosque, built in 996 CE, and the Dongsi Mosque, the oldest mosque in Beijing. The Niujie Mosque today functions as a Qur'an school and an important Islamic studies center. The 500-year-old Dongsi Mosque is built in the architectural style of the Ming dynasty and looks like a Chinese temple. Over the last fifty years, the Chinese government has set aside funds to repair these historic buildings.

In the central province of Henan, where Islam has existed for 1,000 years, some mosques are led by female imams, who study for years to become religious leaders. In that province, a female imam is called an *ahong*. An *ahong* may lead prayers for women, including the prayers of Ramadan.

For decades Chinese Muslims have observed Ramadan without difficulty, but lately the government of China

Muslim worshippers outside of Id Kah Mosque in Kashgar, Xinjiang Province, western China.
iStock.com/Pete Niese

Giza pyramids light up during a sound and light show to celebrate the Ramadan Feast festival in Cairo, Egypt.

Shutterstock.com/mary416

"As we begin Ramadan, I wish all Muslims a blessed time of reflection, family, and good health. Ramadan Mubarak."
—*Hillary Clinton, 2016*

has had an uneasy relationship with its Muslim population. In the province of Xinjiang, where Uighur Muslims form the majority of the population, Uighurs have been discouraged from fasting because the government sees fasting as a sign of dangerous beliefs. Muslim store owners have been ordered to promote the sale of alcohol and cigarettes during Ramadan. While these new regulations make Ramadan more difficult, Muslims in China continue to observe Ramadan and struggle to defend their religious freedom.

Egypt

Egypt is often described as the cultural center of the Arab world, and its traditions influence the entire region. Ramadan is a time of celebration in Egypt. The streets are decorated with Egypt's famous "*fanous* Ramadan" lanterns, which are made of colored glass and tin. (The singular in Arabic is *fanous*, and the plural is *fanawee*.)

Theories about the origins of this tradition vary. Were the lanterns a tradition of Egypt's pharaohs? Or did the custom begin with young boys carrying copper lanterns to chaperone the women of their family during Ramadan? One version of the tradition holds that a **caliph** (a Muslim ruler) was welcomed to Cairo in 969 CE by Egyptians lighting hundreds of lanterns. Another version insists that a different caliph used to venture out into the streets to sight the moon at the beginning of Ramadan, accompanied by children holding lanterns. He ordered all the mosques to light their lanterns with candles during this month. No one knows the origin of the fanous tradition for certain, but today Egyptian children play with their colorful fanawee, singing traditional songs in Arabic, just as they did in the caliph's day.

"Ramadan reminds all of us to… put the needs of others before our own. Let us take the time to recognize…the invaluable contributions of our Muslim communities that enrich our national fabric each and every day. Canada's cultural diversity is one of our greatest strengths and sources of pride."
—*Prime Minister Justin Trudeau, 2016*

Inside Muhammad Ali Mosque in Cairo, Egypt.
Shutterstock.com/aaelrahman89

Another Egyptian Ramadan tradition is the appearance of the Night Caller, or the *Al-Mesarahati*. The Night Caller's role is to walk around Egypt's villages and cities and wake the people for suhoor before the fast. He might call villagers by name, or he might bang his drum loudly in the streets. He wishes those who are fasting a happy Ramadan and encourages them to remember God. At the end of Ramadan Egyptians usually give the Night Caller a gift in gratitude for his efforts.

India

India has a population of 176 million Muslims. In one of India's largest cities, Hyderabad, the Muslim community sacrifices a camel in God's name on the first Friday

People line up to buy fresh dates to break their fast, in the old part of Delhi, India.
iStock.com/BDphoto

of Ramadan. The meat is then given to the poor. Other significant Ramadan foods in India include *haleem*, a porridge-like meal consisting of meat, wheat and lentils, and dozens of different types of *biryanis*, which are rice dishes laced with spices and containing fish, meat, eggs and/or vegetables. Tandoori chicken is also a great favorite.

Breaking the fast inside Istiqlal Mosque, in Jakarta, Indonesia.
iStock.com/PRADEEP87

Indonesia

Indonesia is made up of a chain of islands and has a Muslim population of more than 209 million, the largest of any country. Indonesia is also a melting pot of cultures and languages, so it has many different Ramadan traditions.

Ceremonial musicians announce the beginning of Ramadan by walking through the streets singing hymns and banging drums. In the evenings a drum called a *bedug*

"We join our prayerful good wishes to those of Pope Francis for abundant blessings during Ramadan and for a lasting joy of 'Id [Eid] al-Fitr. Happy Feast to you all!"
—Jean-Louis Cardinal Tauran, President, Pontifical Council for Interreligious Dialogue, 2016

is sounded inside the mosque, inviting Muslims to break their fast. In the month before Ramadan many special Ramadan programs are held, while schoolchildren march in parades around the city. Families visit their deceased loved ones during Ramadan.

Ramadan in Indonesia is also celebrated with festivals and holy rites. In the city of Semarang, on the north coast of the island of Java, a festival called *Dugderan* takes place. The word *dug* represents the sound of the drum that heralds the beginning of Ramadan, while the word *der* refers to the cannon that is fired at the same time as the drum inside the mosque is sounded. A creature that resembles a dragon and leads the carnival is called the *warak ngendog*. Some traditions hold that the warak ngendog is a version of the famous winged creature known as **Buraq** (see sidebar).

Iran

In Iran eating, drinking and smoking are not allowed in public during the month of Ramadan. As in Indonesia and elsewhere, most restaurants and tea houses close, while work hours are shortened to make fasting a little easier. Iranians usually break their fasts with dates and a cup of tea. Ramadan favorites include bread, cheese, and fresh vegetables and fruits. Popular desserts are *zoolbia* and *bamiyeh*, traditional sweets coated in sugar syrup, and *shole zard*, sweet rice made with sugar and saffron.

The majority of Iran's Muslims are **Shia** Muslims. Iranian Shias observe some slight variations in their Ramadan customs. For example, they break their fast a little later in the evening than *Sunni* Muslims, waiting for the sun to set completely.

Ramadan Facts

The Buraq and the Warak Ngendog

Muslims believe that the Prophet Muhammad was once taken on a night journey (*Israa-e-Miraj* in Arabic) through the heavens. The prophet's journey began in the city of Jerusalem at the famous *Dome of the Rock*. The "rock" refers to where the Prophet Muhammad stood to ascend to the heavens. He rode a winged creature called Buraq to complete this important journey. Indonesia's dragon-creature is said to have been inspired by Buraq.

Young women at Imam Square in Isfahan, Iran.

Shutterstock.com/fotosaga

Girls in Kenya, Nairobi.
iStock.com/Melih Cevdet Teksen

Lagos, Nigeria.
iStock.com/Peeter Viisimaa

Kenya

The coastal city of Mombasa, Kenya, comes alive during the month of Ramadan. Most shops and restaurants change their hours to reflect the hours of the fast. The night is especially lively, with street vendors selling many special Ramadan foods, such as *muhogo wa nazi* (cassava in coconut milk), *mbaazi wa nazi* (pigeon peas in coconut milk) and *mahamri* (coconut and cardamom donuts), in areas close to local mosques.

Nigeria

Nigeria is a country in northwest Africa. About half of its population of 182 million people is Muslim, and the other half is Christian. There has been a great deal of civil unrest in Nigeria in recent years, as different communities have been unhappy with their government and sometimes with one another, but Ramadan is still observed punctually. Though government and corporate offices don't close during Ramadan, employers do give their Muslim employees prayer breaks and the opportunity to break their fast at iftar time. Eid-al-Fitr is celebrated as a two-day official holiday in Nigeria.

The price of fruit shoots up during Ramadan, as most Nigerian families prefer to break their fast with fruit. Other iftar foods that are commonly served include corn flour, fried eggs, plantains, bread, fried yams and corn on the cob.

Pakistan

In Pakistan people put up tiny outdoor lights to signal Ramadan, and most restaurants close during the hours of the fast but reopen after iftar. Drummers make the rounds to announce the morning meal, which is called *sehri* in the Urdu language spoken in Pakistan, a variation of the Arabic word *suhoor*. A special tradition of the Indian subcontinent is that women and girls get together for a *chaand raat* party. *Chaand raat* means "night of the moon," and it occurs on the last night of Ramadan. Girls decorate their hands with elaborate henna patterns for Eid morning. After Eid prayer, a special dessert made with boiled milk, sugar and vermicelli noodles is served. This dessert,

"It's about appreciating what you have and having a big celebration at the end, and it makes me feel happy."
—Aleena, age 11

Children at Islamic school in Multan, Pakistan.
Shutterstock.com/thomas koch

Entrance to the Badshahi Mosque, in Lahore, Pakistan. *Shutterstock.com/gaborbasch*

called *savaiyaan*, is often decorated with dates, coconut shavings and pistachios.

Palestine

In Palestine Ramadan is a celebration that focuses on fasting, food, family and the mosque.

In the holy city of Jerusalem (**Al-Quds** in Arabic) the **Masjid Al-Aqsa** is the center of Palestinian life. It is directly across from the majestic Dome of the Rock, one of Islam's holiest sites. (Remember that the Prophet Muhammad's night journey through the heavens began at the Dome of the Rock.) During Ramadan the mosque's courtyard is filled with families who have come to pray. Iftars are held in the courtyard; these communal meals offer the opportunity to feed the hungry, as well as allowing families to enjoy a sense of community.

"It was really great to celebrate Ramadan in Pakistan one year. Everyone was in the same boat as me when I was fasting. When Eid came, lights were hung everywhere just like Christmas lights."
—*Irfan, age 12*

Picnicking is a very common way for Palestinians to celebrate the end of each fast. Although life is very difficult under the Israeli Occupation, Palestinian families celebrate the end of each fast by engaging in public life as much as they are able, visiting friends and neighbors, sharing food, and going to markets, parks or the sea, when there are no curfews or travel restrictions.

What is remarkable about Palestinian culture is the food that is central to Ramadan. In some small towns, a drum is played to wake people up for suhoor. The morning meal in Palestine includes a combination of *hawadeh* (ready foods) and *nawashef* (dry foods without sauce). These can include hummus, falafel, olives, eggplants stuffed with nuts, grilled Nablusi cheese, *zaatar* (a combination of herbs, salt and sesame seeds) and *lebneh* (a soft cream cheese made from strained yogurt). For the evening

The best-known Ramadan dessert in Palestine is kuttayif, a stuffed pastry with walnuts and cinnamon, or cheese, drenched in a delicious sugar-lemon syrup.

Masjid Al-Aqsa.
Shutterstock.com/SeanPavonePhoto

> "I love knowing that even if our traditions are different, there's a whole community of Muslims sharing this month of fasting all around the world."
> —Mazin, age 15

meal, dates are always on the table, and it's common to begin with a vegetable or chicken broth. Palestinian families also serve *fatteh*, platters layered with rice or bread, and meat and vegetables. Stuffed vegetables, rolled leaves and a wide variety of soups are also made especially for Ramadan, and carob juice is a popular drink. Ring-shaped sesame seed breads called *kaek bi simsim* are a Jerusalem specialty during Ramadan, and *baraze* cookies are another popular treat. In the crowded bazaars of the old city of Jerusalem, vendors can often be heard calling out, "*Kaek, kaek*," which lets people know that fresh kaek bi simsim sesame seed bread is available.

Children taking off their shoes at the entrance of the Al-Aqsa Mosque in Jerusalem.
Shutterstock.com/aicragarual

The Ka'bah mosque in Mecca, Saudi Arabia.
Shutterstock.com/hikrcn

Saudi Arabia

Many Muslims in Saudi Arabia congregate in Mecca, the birthplace of the Prophet Muhammad. At the center of Mecca is a cubelike structure called the ***Ka'bah***, which is covered with a black cloth inscribed with verses of the Qur'an. Muslims believe the Ka'bah was originally built by Abraham. When the Prophet Muhammad was chosen to deliver the message of Islam, all Muslims were told to pray in the direction of Mecca, facing the Ka'bah. Before this, Muslims used to pray in the direction of Jerusalem. During Ramadan, the mosque of the Ka'bah is filled with worshippers observing their five daily prayers. A beautiful recitation of the Qur'an can be heard at the mosque of the Ka'bah during Ramadan.

Young women in Khartoum, Sudan.
iStock.com/kertu_ee

Sudan

Sudan is one of the largest countries in Africa, with a population of 42 million. A diverse society made up of many different cultures and ethnicities, the people of Sudan are famous for their hospitality during Ramadan: open-air iftars are a deeply rooted tradition. Travelers on the road are invited to rest and join these communal iftars, as offering food to others who are fasting is considered a noble act.

Turkey

In Turkey the **minarets** of mosques are decorated with lights called *mahya*. They display religious messages that capture the spirit of Ramadan. Turkish families host many iftar parties during Ramadan, and the menu is packed with sweets. Ramadan specialties include *gullac* (layers of pastry soaked in rosewater-milk), *kadayif dolma* (a walnut-filled pastry), *revani* (sponge cakes soaked in syrup), baklava and Turkish delight. During the month of fasting, restaurants offer special Ramadan menus.

"It feels like these days we don't have a lot to celebrate. So getting together for Eid is a day when we don't worry about all the bad news. We get to be happy instead."
—*Dima, age 13*

When making this recipe as well as the other recipes in this book, be sure an adult is around to supervise.

TANDOORI CHICKEN ON A SKEWER

Tandoori chicken is a popular dish from the Indian subcontinent and is usually made in a tandoor oven. This recipe is a simple variation that cooks in 25 minutes and serves as a main course.

Ingredients:

½ cup plain yogurt
2 to 3 tablespoons tandoori masala
1 teaspoon salt
3 chicken breasts, cubed
Wooden or metal skewers

Directions:

In a large dish, thoroughly mix together the yogurt, masala and salt. Place the chicken cubes in the yogurt mixture, cover the dish with plastic wrap and marinate for 10 minutes in the fridge.

Preheat the oven to 400 degrees F. Remove the chicken from the fridge and push chicken pieces onto the skewers. Cover a baking tray or pan with tinfoil and set the skewers on the tray. Bake for 20 to 25 minutes, turning chicken over at the halfway point.

Variation: Marinate mushrooms and pieces of onion or bell pepper in the masala mixture, and add them to the skewers.

Dunya's Story

Dunya is an 11-year-old Palestinian girl who lives in East Jerusalem with her parents and five brothers and sisters. Every weekend she walks with her family through the streets of the Old City to the courtyard of the Dome of the Rock. Often she joins in Friday prayer with the congregation, but sometimes she likes to pray by herself at the dome so she can sit next to the famous surface of the rock and lean over to touch it. She imagines what it would be like to ride a winged creature named Buraq up into the heavens.

After the Friday prayer, she rejoins her family for a picnic out in the courtyard. Her favorite part of the picnic is getting to peel and eat delicious Palestinian oranges in the shadow of the golden dome. The dome reflects the history and heritage of her people, and Dunya feels a thrill of pride and joy whenever she is near it.

The Dome of the Rock
in Jerusalem.
iStock.com/kirill4mula

A final word from the author

Ramadan has been a part of my life since my early childhood. Though many people think of fasting as a hardship, I greet the arrival of Ramadan each year with a sense of joy and celebration. I look at Ramadan as an opportunity to change and grow, and to strive to become a better person. I like the sense of personal challenge it offers, as well as the deeply rooted spiritual comfort I find during this month. I feel connected not only to the legacy of the Islamic civilization throughout its history, but also to my Muslim brothers and sisters all around the world, who color the month of Ramadan with the beauty of their own traditions. Best of all, I like seeing how young people are putting the principles of Ramadan into action in their communities by finding new ways to help others.

A note from the series editor

"The Origins are built on the bedrock of personal stories, enhanced by careful research and illuminated by stunning photographs. No book can be all things to all people, and no two people experience a culture in the same way. The Origins are not meant to be the definitive word on any culture or belief; instead they will lead readers toward a place where differences are acknowledged and knowledge facilitates understanding."

—Sarah N. Harvey

Zayna and Maysa Khan relax in the garden before Eid prayers.

Athif Ali Khan

GLOSSARY

Allah—the name for God in Arabic

Al-Quds—the Arabic name for Jerusalem

the Ansar (the Helpers)—the people who received the Prophet Muhammad in Medina

Ashra—one of three ten-day parts of the month of Ramadan

Buraq—the winged creature that the Prophet Muhammad rode in his night journey through the heavens

caliph—a Muslim ruler

Dome of the Rock—a holy site in Jerusalem, where the Prophet Muhammad stood to ascend to the heavens

Eid-al-Fitr (Eid)—the Festival of Breaking the Fast, which marks the end of Ramadan

Eid Mubarak—the traditional Eid greeting, meaning "blessed celebration" or "may your Eid be blessed"

Fajr—the morning prayer

genocide—deliberate measures taken with the intent to destroy a group of people who are targeted because of their race, religion, or national or ethnic identity

Grand Mufti—the highest religious leader in a Sunni Muslim country

Hafiz/Hafiza—someone who has memorized the whole Qur'an (a Hafiz is male and a Hafiza is female)

Hajj—one of the five pillars of Islam; a pilgrimage to Mecca

halal—food prepared in accordance with Muslim dietary laws

Hira—the cave where the Angel Gabriel delivered the message of Islam to the Prophet Muhammad

iftar—the meal that breaks the fast each day during Ramadan

imam—the leader of a Muslim congregation

Islam—a monotheistic religion with more than 1.6 billion followers worldwide

Ka'bah—a cubelike structure at the center of Mecca, which Muslims believe was built by Abraham

khutbah—a sermon offered at Friday prayer and also as part of the Eid prayer

Koran—another spelling of Qur'an, the holy book of Islam

Laylat-al-Qadr—the Arabic term for the Night of Destiny or Night of Power (called Shub-e-Qadr in Urdu and in Persian, or Farsi)

lunar calendar—a calendar based on the moon's orbit of Earth, rather than Earth's orbit of the sun

Maghrib—the short prayer performed at dusk

Masjid Al-Aqsa—a mosque across from the Dome of the Rock in Jerusalem

Mecca—a holy city of Islam where the Prophet Muhammad was born

Medina—the city where the Prophet Muhammad sought refuge from persecution, and where he later died

minaret—a slender tower attached to a mosque, from which Muslims are called to prayer

monotheistic religion—a religion that holds that there is only one god

mosque (*masjid*)—a Muslim house of worship where Muslims go to pray

Muhammad—the prophet or messenger of God who received the divine revelation of the Qur'an; he was born in Mecca around 570 CE

Muslim—a follower of the religion of Islam

Night of Destiny/Night of Power—the holiest night of the year for Muslims, occurring in the last ten days of Ramadan

persecution—the oppression or abuse of people because of their religion, beliefs or other characteristics

prophet—a person who is a messenger of God and reveals His will

Qur'an—the holy book of Islam

Ramadan—the holy month of fasting for Muslims

sadaqa—a form of giving that Muslims participate in throughout the year, including during Ramadan

Salah—one of the five pillars of Islam; prayer

Sawm—one of the five pillars of Islam; fasting during the holy month of Ramadan

secede—to withdraw from an organization or country

Shahadah—one of the five pillars of Islam; the act of bearing witness to the Oneness of God

Shia—a member of one of the two main branches of Islam, who believes that after the Prophet Muhammad's death, his son-in-law and cousin Ali was the rightful leader of the Muslim community, giving Ali a unique spiritual authority that passed on to his descendants

solar calendar—a calendar whose dates indicate the position of the Earth on its revolution around the sun, or the apparent position of the sun moving on the celestial sphere

suhoor—the pre-dawn meal before the daily fast begins during Ramadan

Sunni— a member of one of the two main branches of Islam; Sunnis recognize and accept the first four caliphs (or leaders of the Muslim community) after the Prophet Muhammad's death; both Sunnis and Shias follow the teachings and practice of the Prophet Muhammad, though they may interpret these teachings differently

Taraweeh prayers—special evening prayers performed during Ramadan, in addition to the five daily prayers

Zakah—one of the five pillars of Islam; giving to charity every year

zakat-al-fitr—a small donation that all Muslims make on Eid day

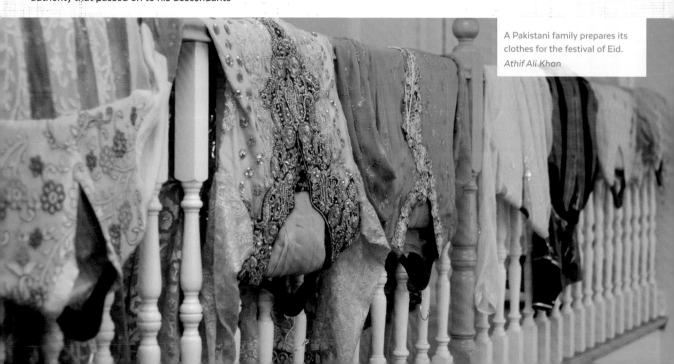

A Pakistani family prepares its clothes for the festival of Eid.
Athif Ali Khan

RESOURCES

Chapter One

Online:

The Huffington Post: A Quick Lesson about Ramadan, the Muslim Month of Fasting.
http://www.huffingtonpost.com/entry/a-quick-lesson-about-ramadan-the-muslim-month-of-fasting_us_574dde8ee4b0af73af959819

Medical News Today: Fasting: Health Benefits and Risks. www.medicalnewstoday.com/articles/295914.php

Koran by Heart (documentary film). www.youtube.com/watch?v=ptHdmw57rzM

The Huffington Post: What It's Like to Train for the Olympics While Fasting for Ramadan.
www.huffingtonpost.com/entry/ibtihaj-muhammad-ramadan-olympics_us_5761b5b8e4b09c926cfe07db

Chapter Two

Print:

Sharif, Medeia. *Bestest. Ramadan. Ever.* Woodbury, MN: Flux, 2011.

Understanding the Month of Glory: Lessons on the Month of Ramadan. www.al-islam.org/printpdf/book/export/html/18111

Online:

IslamiCity: Ramadan. www.islamicity.org/topics/ramadan

The New York Times: Teenage Summer, the Fasting Version. www.nytimes.com/2010/08/21/nyregion/21bigcity.html

Watercolor Moods blog: The Teen's Guide to Islam: Ramadan. watercolormoods.blogspot.com/2015/06/the-teens-guide-to-islam-ramadan.html

Chapter Three

Online:

Next Wave Muslim Initiative: Camp Next Wave Muslim Initiative (Camp Ramadan).
www.nextwavemuslims.org

Al Arabiya English: Charity in Ramadan Explained: Giving Up Food, Giving Back to Society.
https://english.alarabiya.net/en/2015/06/26/Charity-in-Ramadan-Giving-up-food-
giving-back-to-society.html

GIVE 30: www.give30.org

Project Downtown. www.projectdowntown.org

Ramadan Tent Project blog. https://ramadantentproject.wordpress.com/

Chapter Four

Online:

Festival Sherpa: 10 Beautiful Ramadan Traditions from Around the World. www.festivalsherpa.com/
10-beautiful-ramadan-traditions-around-world/

Fordson: Faith, Fasting and Football (documentary film). www.fordsonthemovie.com/

True Tube: Great British Ramadan (video). www.truetube.co.uk/film/great-british-ramadan

How Stuff Works: How Ramadan Works. people.howstuffworks.com/culture-traditions/
holidays-other/ramadan2

Unity Productions Foundation: Nadia's Ramadan (short film). www.upf.tv/nadiasramadan/

Reuters: Ramadan: Iftar around the World (slideshow). https://widerimage.reuters.com/story/
ramadan-iftar-around-the-world

INDEX

Page numbers in **bold** indicate an image; there may also be text related to the same topic on that page

Acknowledgments

Thank you to Sarah Harvey for asking me to take on this wonderful project. I'm so fortunate to have benefited from her encouragement and guidance. Thank you to everyone at Orca Book Publishers for publishing such a worthwhile and necessary series. Thank you to Robin Stevenson for being so generous with her time and help, and for her amazing book *Pride: Celebrating Diversity & Community*. Thank you to my fellow authors in this series for blazing a trail.

My deep gratitude to Shaikh Ahmed Kutty for reading over this manuscript—it wouldn't be what it is without his wisdom and insight. Thank you to my dear friends Sajidah Kutty and Uzma Jalaluddin for answering all my questions—they are my go-to Ramadan girls. My warmest appreciation to Rabbi Avram Mlotek and Josh Getzler for such a lovely and meaningful conversation on the traditions we hold in common. I'm deeply grateful to Sahar Mustafah for her advice on Palestinian life and for so graciously proofreading my efforts.

Thank you to all my friends and family who helped get their kids involved in this book, but especially to Nozhat Choudry, Uzma Alam, Iram Ahmed and Najia Usman for going above and beyond; the amazing kids who chimed in on what Ramadan means to them; my wonderful nieces—Summer Shaikh, for her invaluable research assistance and her help with photography, and Noor Shaikh, for taking so many gorgeous photographs; Fereshteh Hashemi for her great suggestions and for arranging her dinner table so beautifully; and my cousin Athif Khan for his beautiful photographs of Eid. And thank you to my parents, siblings and husband—I've celebrated my happiest Ramadans with you—and Danielle Burby, my personal dragon-slayer.

Finally, I'd like to acknowledge the efforts of all the kids I know who dedicate themselves to the spirit and purpose of Ramadan, and to the ones who will grow up to join them in their efforts: Summer, Casim, Layth, Maysa, Zayna, Noor, Negean, Ameer, Amin, Naseem, Iman, Nadia, Zahra, Hanna, Maariya, Zain, Safiya, Aydin, Ayla and Adalynn.

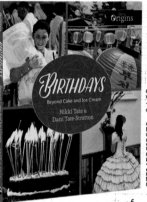